T0105892

Milet Publishing
Smallfields Cottage, Cox Green
Rudgwick, Horsham, West Sussex
RH12 3DE England
info@milet.com
www.milet.com
www.milet.co.uk

First English–French edition published by Milet Publishing in 2013

Copyright © Milet Publishing, 2013

ISBN 978 1 84059 792 9

Original Turkish text written by Erdem Seçmen
Translated to English by Alvin Parmar and adapted by Milet

Illustrated by Chris Dittopoulos
Designed by Christangelos Seferiadis

Printed and bound in Turkey by Ertem Matbaası

My Bilingual Book

Sight

La vue

English–French

How do we see colors on a butterfly's wings?

Comment perçoit-on les couleurs des ailes d'un papillon ?

Let's think about how we see things . . .

Réfléchissons à la façon dont nous voyons les choses . . .

Our eyes show us everything, like faces,

Nos yeux nous montrent tout : les visages,

colors, actions, places . . .

les couleurs, les actions, les lieux . . .

Giraffe has a coat of brown spots on yellow.

La girafe porte un manteau jaune à pois bruns.

Watch him bend to say hello!

Regarde-là se pencher pour te saluer !

Our eyes can show our feelings.

Nos yeux peuvent trahir nos sentiments.

We see Panda's eyes are smiling.

Regarde le sourire dans les yeux du panda.

To see, we need more than our eyes.

Pour voir, nos yeux ne suffisent pas.

We need light at night to help us spy.

La nuit, nous avons besoin de lumière pour voir.

Owl can see in a different way.

Le hibou voit de façon différente.

Even in the dark, he can spot his prey.

Même dans le noir, il peut repérer sa proie.

Seeing through glasses? Now I'm perplexed!

Tu portes des lunettes ? Me voilà perplexe !

When our eyes need help, we give them specs!

Quand nos yeux ont besoin d'aide, nous leur offrons des lunettes !

Tears are not only for sad or happy,

Les larmes ne servent pas qu'à pleurer de chagrin ou de joie,

they help keep our eyes moist and healthy.

elles permettent à nos yeux de rester humides et en bonne santé.

Our eyelids spread our tears when we blink,

Nos paupières chassent les larmes quand nous clignons des yeux,

and we use them to sleep and to wink!

nous les utilisons pour dormir et faire des clins d'œil !

We close our eyes when we're asleep in bed,

Nous fermons les yeux lorsque nous dormons,

but in our dreams, we may see orange, green, red . . .

s dans nos rêves nous pouvons voir du rouge, du vert, de l'orange . . .